WESTERN AMERICA

EVERGREEN is an imprint of Benedikt Taschen Verlag GmbH

© for this edition: 1998 Benedikt Taschen Verlag GmbH
Hohenzollernring 53, D–50672 Köln
© 1996 Editions du Chêne – Hachette Livre – L'Ouest Américain
Under the direction of Michel Buntz – Hoa Qui Photographic Agency
Editor: Corinne Fossey
Maps and illustrations: Jean-Michel Kirsch
Text: Jean-Yves Montagu
Photographs: Alain Thomas
Cover: Angelika Taschen, Cologne
Translated by Andrew Wilson
In association with First Edition Translations Ltd, Cambridge
Realization of the English edition by First Edition Translations Ltd, Cambridge

Printed in Italy
ISBN 3-8228-7755-7

WESTERN AMERICA

THE NATIONAL PARKS

Text JEAN-YVES MONTAGU
Photographs ALAIN THOMAS

EVERGREEN

Under a cloudless sky, a vast expanse of land stretches out before me to the clear horizon. The tops of the mountains sparkle in the setting sun. The wind has just veered northwards. I have the impression that a huge bird is circling the camp, pushing against the advancing night. I have the dizzying feeling of being at the centre of the world's mysteries and can hear my own breathing. I am drifting towards I know not what far-off places on the edge of the Rockies. I recall the words of Nathaniel Hawthorne (American writer, 1804–1864) in *The House of the Seven Gables*: "Where is our universe? All crumbled away from us, and we, adrift in chaos, may hearken to the gusts of homeless wind, that go sighing and murmuring about in quest of what was once a world!" Today, there are precisely seven peaks of light encircling me, seven specks of fire gleaming against the black coat of the night that quivers like the back of a coyote preparing to devour a carcass. I will leave it to the reader to judge the value of these correspondences. They have something of the feel of symbols looming up to mark out the frontier between the spiritual and the earthly.

For three days, three days of slow, secret rituals, I have been making my way down into the heart of the natural world. This evening, I have clad myself in stars in order to hear what the darkness tells me. Despite the immensity of the place, the light is like that in a cloister. Why is a wall always necessary in order to send back an echo? "What is the Western frontier? Undoubtedly no two people will have the same understanding of what it is. The term may be in widespread use, but for everyone, from the President to the humblest farmer, it evokes only a vague image of a place over there in the West, of an ill-defined frontier between civilization and barbarism." These are the words of Colonel Dodge. At the end of the last century, it fell to this military officer to conduct negotiations with the Indians over territories that the Gold Rush had just turned into battlefields. Take good note of the words "civilization and barbarism". This was how the frontier was defined a century ago, when the "Great Spirit Chief" was spitting out orders like withered snake skins. The prairie shuddered and the wind brought only words of vengeance and death, for the white man was advancing inexorably towards the Pacific. For the American Census Office, this Western frontier corresponded to an area in which the density of population was between two and six inhabitants per square mile.

The year 1890 saw the official disappearance of this boundary between civilization and barbarism, which had shifted continuously from the beginning of the seventeenth century to the end of the nineteenth century as the white man moved westwards. The great leap forward took place after the discovery in 1848 of extensive gold deposits in California, a discovery which was to trigger the integration of the Far West into the nascent United States of America.

Nevertheless, another source of inspiration, ecologically aware and rooted in a universal poetics and humanism, was to emerge at the same time as the economic and political desires for domination. Indeed, while the conquest of the West contained within it the seeds of the American myth of triumphant capitalism, the equally fundamental myth of respect for the environment was to crystallize in the American consciousness during the same period.

John Muir, the inspiration behind the American national parks movement, proclaimed in 1868, as he contemplated the unviolated splendours of Yosemite Valley: "As long as I live, I'll hear waterfalls and birds and winds sing. I'll interpret the rocks, learn the language of flood, storm, and the avalanche. I'll acquaint myself with the glaciers and wild gardens, and get as near the heart of the world as I can. And what should I care about hunger, cold, hard labour, poverty, solitude, money, the desire to be famous or to get married." His articles, which were published in *Century Magazine*, were to have a decisive impact on Congress. In May 1903, Theodore Roosevelt came to camp for four days with him in the famous valley. "Four of the most beautiful days of my life," he said afterwards. The President of the United States was later to say of this legendary character, who is still the most commemorated individual in the state of California: "The freest man I have ever met".

*O*verleaf: the American West offers a very wide range of spectacular landscapes, but the Rocky Mountains are a constant presence. This backbone of the American continent, stretching from Patagonia to Alaska, was formed some 65 million years ago. In Alberta, glaciers feed milky-blue lakes. Moraine Lake in Banff National Park.

This evening, I can almost hear the voice of old John. "To allow oneself to be permeated by the song of the universe, that is what matters," he used to say before going to sleep. The camp is now buried in the dark of the great American night, with its canopy of stars. The sky looks like a silent flag studded with flowers. Firmly wedged in my sandstone armchair, I observe its flappings. The void is filled with silent presences. I am writing from a frontier located within a labyrinth where there is no trace of man. I feel as though I have plummeted like a stone into the heart of a secret that has enveloped me in its mysteries. However, before the sun fell behind the horizon, I had time to seize its last ray, the one that the Indians say is the string on which the Great Spirit Chief plays music. Today, in the age of the laptop, it is in the heart of the Far West that his music, the song of the universe, is to be heard.

Death Valley – a trough in the tectonic plate – gradually turned to desert following the retreat of the sea 65 million years ago. The various sedimentary strata now form lunar-like landscapes as at Zabriskie Point shown opposite.

In the northern Rockies, from the Yukon to Alaska, along the Dempter Highway, the flowering of the fireweed heralds the arrival of spring, suffusing the spongy tundra and the undergrowth of the coniferous forests with pink.

The Rockies run the whole length of Western America, a common feature around which an infinite range of landscapes jostle with each other. They are young mountains, uplifted only 65 million years ago as the tectonic plates came together, causing the land suddenly to rise up. Under this intense pressure, the land rose to a height of 1,600 metres (5,250 feet), forming a vast plateau stretching from Colorado to California and from New Mexico to Montana. At the same time, the movement of faults in the earth's crust caused a large number of peaks to soar more than 4,000 metres (13,000 feet) into the sky, particularly in Colorado and Wyoming, as well as in Southern Alaska and the Yukon, where Mount McKinley, at a height of 6,200 metres (20,320 feet), stands supreme. These mountainous regions have long been the location of national forests and national parks – Rocky Mountain, Grand Teton, Glacier, North Cascades. Seen through the eyes of an eagle circling overhead, autumn in these regions creates some spectacular sights. From the end of August, it first carpets the tundra in purple heather and then descends through the forests of maple, pine, oak and spruce as far as Northern Arizona, coating the mountainsides with the gold of the aspens.

The most beautiful glacier lakes are in Canada, but unfortunately many have been spoilt by tourist developments. Those seeking nature unsullied by human intervention have to go to Alaska. The photographs on this page show Portage Glacier in Chugach National Forest.
Overleaf: Mount McKinley in Denali National Park is the highest peak in Northern America.

Olympic National Park, on the Olympic Peninsula south of Vancouver, has an abundance of torrents and waterfalls. The park is essentially a temperate rainforest; its highest point is Mount Olympus, which rises to a height of 2,430 m (7,976 ft).

You may have heard of the stories of Blue Jay. They are tales similar to La Fontaine's fables that the Indians of the Northwest of the United States used to tell when storms prevented them from putting to sea to hunt whales. One of the tribes, the Makahs, had become experts in harpooning these enormous creatures as they made their way along the Pacific Coast. Their method was simple. They got as close as possible to the animal before stabbing it with harpoons to which they had attached inflated water skins, which prevented the creature from diving swiftly down into the depths. The struggle could last for several days. The hunters' zeal for their task was sustained by songs, which gave a certain rhythm to the men's efforts. The whales themselves became the objects of a genuine cult. The songs the whalers sang told of the birth of a very rare species in immaculate shells the colour of the stars. In other songs, these shells were blue, like the sky and the jay of the fable.

A funny bird, Blue Jay! Rowdy, boastful and scheming, he used to stir up ill-feeling everywhere. He was, as it were, the gods' licensed

Although its climate is temperate, the forest of the Olympic National Park, with its rich diversity of plants, lichens, and mosses, has certain similarities with forests nearer the Equator.

Overleaf: thousands of tree trunks ripped from the forest by torrents are strewn along the west coast of the Olympic Peninsula. It is not unusual to see schools of grey whales from these shingle beaches.

fool; the sparrow hawk, whom Blue Jay ridiculed regularly as he shot like an arrow through the hawk's hunting territory, complained that he was a "spoilsport". "You're a cheeky little rascal," he would say to Blue Jay, who would regularly silence him with his old squaw's cackle. Imagine the atmosphere around the fire when the tribes' storytellers gathered for verbal sparring matches, which were in fact real dramatic events, for Blue Jay had an older brother, Robin Redbreast, who used to lecture him regularly in sententious tones. The account of Blue Jay's innumerable pranks makes up an anthology that the Indians handed down from generation to generation. These fables were both educative and poetic. They were the cultural glue of a community that lived on the peninsula between the Pacific Ocean to the west and Juan de Fuca Strait to the north. Puget Sound, to the east, is an arm of the sea strewn with islands that separates it from the Seattle peninsula. It is a wild region, austere and hard, isolated from the mainland by Mount Olympus. It has an atmosphere redolent of Herman Melville's account in *Moby Dick* of the legend of how the island of Nantucket, on the northeast coast of the United

States, was settled by Indians: in olden times an eagle swooped down upon the New England coast, and carried off an infant Indian in his talons. With loud lament the parents saw their child borne out of sight over the wide waters. They resolved to follow in the same direction. Setting out in their canoes, after a perilous passage they discovered the island, and there they found an empty ivory casket containing the poor little Indian's skeleton.

What wonder, then, that these Nantucketers, born on a beach, should take to the sea for a livelihood … and declared everlasting war with the mightiest animated mass that has survived the flood; most monstrous and most mountainous! That Himmalehan, salt-sea Mastodon, clothed with such portentousness of unconscious power, that his very panics are more to be dreaded than his most fearless and malicious assaults!

In Yellowstone National Park, which lies in a caldera some 8,990 km² (3,472 square miles) in area, all the main geysers have names.
Right: Castle Geyser, with its curious siliceous protuberance.

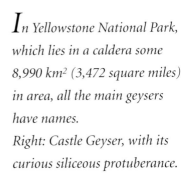

Situated in the northwest of Wyoming and spilling over slightly into Idaho and Montana, Yellowstone National Park is not only the first national park to have been established in the world but also the largest in the United States. It covers an area of 8,990 km² (3,472 square miles). The park lies in the heart of the Rocky Mountains, in a region of spectacular scenery criss-crossed by winding but magnificent roads at heights of between 2,000 and 2,700 metres (6,550 and 8,850 feet). It is also an area of intense geological activity. At Yellowstone, the earth's crust, which floats on a turbulent mass of boiling lava, is only 5 kilometres (3 miles) deep; in other continental regions, it has an average thickness of 50 kilometres (31 miles)! As a result, water heated by volcanic rocks erupts intermittently at the surface as hot springs. The 200 geysers in Yellowstone are the largest in the world; only in Iceland and New Zealand is there anything comparable.

An average annual rainfall of 100 centimetres (39 inches) creates a conjunction of forces that gives rise to strange phenomena within the fissures of the earth. While the water stored at the bottom of the geyser column cannot reach boiling point because the pressure is too high, the water in the middle section is heated and turned into steam, which is blasted upwards as a boiling fountain. The cycle starts once more when a new supply of water reaches the depths of the fissures, where the proximity of the molten magma causes the reaction to begin all over again.

Access to the main points of interest in the park can be gained from the Grand Loop Road, which snakes for 235 kilometres (150 miles) in a figure-of-eight shape. Three days are required to cover the route by car. In July and August, this very busy road is often blocked by animals – Yellowstone is the largest animal reserve in the United States after Alaska.

Foremost of these animals is the bear; there are estimated to be 650 brown bears and 350 grizzlies in the park. Nevertheless, they are rarely seen, although before 1970 whole families of bears used to gather to be fed by tourists.

There are also bison. Despite their systematic slaughter by white settlers at the end of the last century, American ecologists did manage to save a few herds. In 1902, two semi-domesticated herds were returned to a ranch in the Lamar Valley, but it was not until 1936 that bison were set free to live in the wild. Today, the Yellowstone herd numbers some 1,000 animals scattered over three main regions: Lamar, Pelican and Hayden Valley, and Firehole. The best time to observe these superb animals is in the winter and spring,

*A*lthough they are less spectacular than the geysers that intermittently spew jets of hot water and steam over 60 m (196 ft) into the air, hot springs sculpt the surrounding ground with delicately coloured deposits of minerals. Some of them, such as the terraces of the Mammoth Hot Springs, form waterfalls that tumble downwards over steps made up of the limestone deposited by the water.

*F*ollowing violent volcanic activity some 600,000 years ago, the Yellowstone River, which flows along the edge of the caldera, opened the way for the forces of erosion to create magnificent canyons with dizzying waterfalls like the Lower Falls (94 m/308 ft).

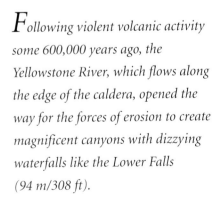

*A*merican cow elk, the name given to the female American elk, graze on the banks of the Firehole River. There are some 20,000 in Yellowstone National Park. It is not unusual to see them in the company of a few solitary bison.

right up until June. Although a few males can be seen in July, August and September, they do not begin to come down to lower ground again until after mid-September. Aficionados should hardly need reminding that the animals should always be approached upwind. The American elk, or wapiti, has a particular liking for Yellowstone, and there are estimated to be some 20,000 of them in the park. It is considerably larger than the European species, both in height and in the size of its antlers. Whole herds gather along the rivers, between the geysers of the Norris Basin and the Mammoth Hot Springs. The sight is unchanging. The males with their imposing, much-branched antlers stay together, except during the rutting period, while the females urge their offspring to walk ahead of them.

The American moose, known as the elk in Europe and Asia, is a powerful beast, not very beautiful but utterly majestic, with its fawn-coloured coat, massive, somewhat disproportionate head, and its long beard, which moves to the rhythm of the animal's continuous rumination. As John Muir used to say, "At Yellowstone, the slightest discovery becomes an event".

The American elk (the male is known as a bull wapiti) reaches a height of 1.50 m (5 ft), measured from the front foot to the shoulder, and can weigh up to 450 kg (990 lb).

If the Far West embodies the notion of infinity, then its lakes take us into another, equally fundamental dimension: depth. Crater Lake is an astonishing site. The immense, midnight-blue lake glistens like a jewel lying in a casket of snow. The contrast is striking. Here, in a strange encounter, the primeval world enters into dialogue with the eternal. The essence of that dialogue is contained in the untroubled expanse of the lake which, as in a dream, seeps into the consciousness like a stream destined to flow until it disappears in the cold, blue light of eternity. Crater Lake is a seminal dream that allows us to glimpse the mystery of the primordial world. To reach it at dawn, as the dew is distilling droplets of freshly resurrected water, is to enter fully into that dream.

Crater Lake National Park covers an area of 649 km² (250 square miles). It is situated in the northwest of the state of Oregon, in the Cascades Range. The forests of Oregon contain more than a dozen species of tree, notably the hemlock spruce, which is highly prized by Japanese decorative artists, the sitka spruce, which is used to make plywood, and the white cedar, which is used for building

While Yellowstone is undoubtedly the focus of volcanic activity in Western America, the rest of the region bears the scars of vulcanism. In the Cascade Range, which runs from northern California to the south of British Columbia, there are some 15 volcanoes, including Mount St Helens, which last exploded with devastating force on 18 May 1980. Mount Mazama, the site of Crater Lake, has been quiescent for 6,800 years.

*O*nce the caldera had cooled down sufficiently, a lake began to form, fed by rainwater and melting snow. It stands at an altitude of 1,900 m (6,232 ft) but never freezes over because of the solar energy stored in its water. Inside the circular caldera, which is some 10 km (6.25 miles) in diameter, stands Wizard Island, a cone of rock that predates the lake; it was formed by one of the many smaller eruptions that followed the major explosion.

boats. However, the most widespread species is the Douglas fir, whose lightness and strength are universally recognized. It grows rapidly, reaching a height of between 45 and 60 metres (148 to 197 feet) in 100 years.

The lake itself, which covers an area of 56 km² (21.3 square miles) in area, occupies the crater of an extinct volcano called Mount Mazama. About 6,000 years ago, the rounded peak of the mountain collapsed under its own weight during an eruption, creating an almost circular basin 11 kilometres (6.85 miles) in diameter and 1,200 metres (3,935 feet) deep. The lake originally had no marine life in it at all. Today, there are various species of trout and salmon in the lake, although the lack of vegetation limits their reproduction. The water of Crater Lake brings to mind not only death, in all its beauty and faithfulness, but also that limpid spirit of the water which, crystallized by inspiration, gave birth to the Word.

Thousands of kilometres of trails allow hikers to discover the unsullied natural world of the Sierra Nevada, where the frail dogwood contrasts with the mighty sequoia.

Four thousand years ago, the Miwok Indians lived contentedly in the deep, fertile, meadowlike Ahwahnee Valley – the Yosemite Valley of today – which nestles between the almost vertical walls of the Sierra Nevada. In 1849, thousands of gold diggers arrived at the foot of the Sierra. Fearing that they would be overwhelmed by the large numbers of prospectors, the Indians attacked the fort of John Savage, a wealthy merchant who sold supplies to the miners. This was the beginning of a war that would end, as it did everywhere, in victory for the white man.

In 1864, a journalist named Greely discovered Yosemite Forest: "The Sierra Nevada does not, it is true, have the magnificent glaciers, the frequent rainfalls, the lush greenery or the numerous waterfalls of the Alps, but it surpasses all other mountain ranges in its variety of species. From whatever peak one surveys the landscape, one's gaze feeds always on an uninterrupted ocean of luxuriant greenery stretching away endlessly into the distance, covering all the valleys of the high plateaux, all the slopes and all the peaks, with the exception of the very highest, with its persistent opulence.

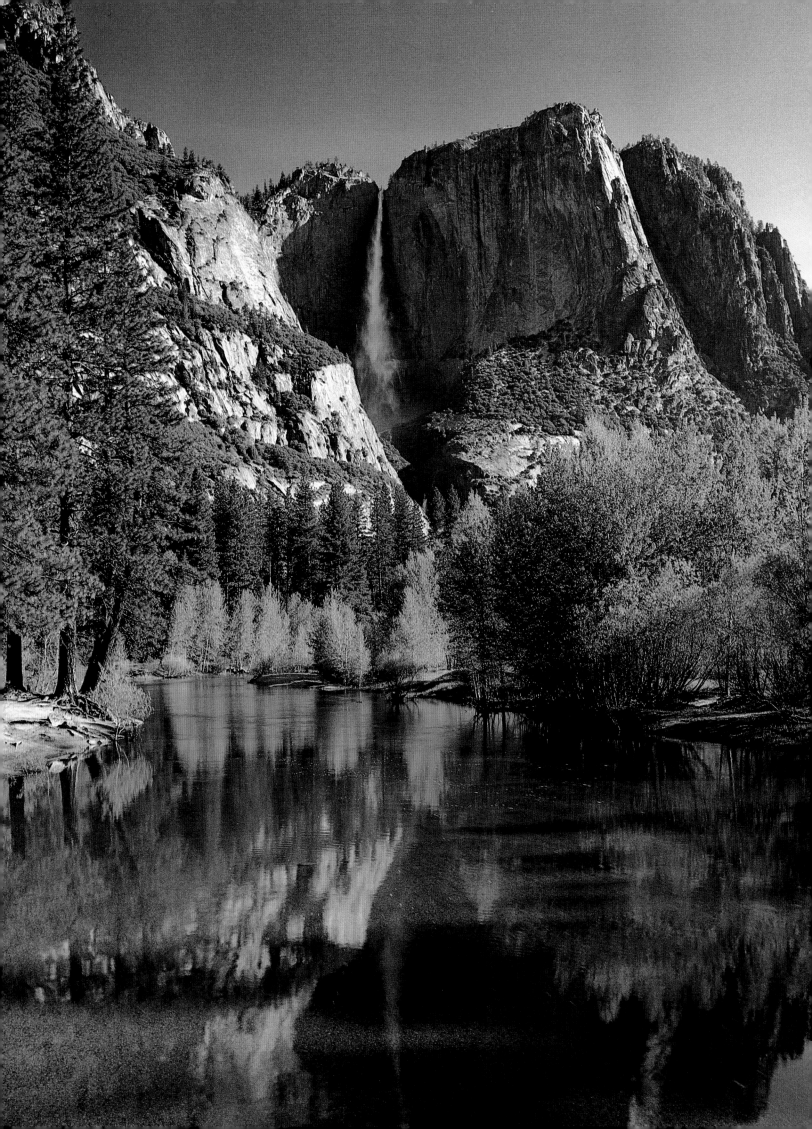

In the course of today's journey, I saw hundreds of pines with trunks eight feet in diameter, and most certainly cedars as well at least six feet in diameter. I saw mile after mile of trees of this size and others of the same species, but smaller, of exactly the thickness that their environment allows. It would seem that the steep slopes, where they grow in tiered rows without depriving each other of sunlight, are particularly favourable to these useful giants. However, the meadows of the upper slopes are bordered splendidly by various kinds of balsam firs, some barely a foot in diameter, others almost two hundred high, their branches surrounding them like a ruff that the weight of the winter snow has turned elegantly down, which make them undoubtedly, as seen here, one of the most beautiful trees in the world. The foothills that separate these meadows from each other are also covered by a species of pine which, as far as elegance is concerned, concedes virtually nothing to the firs we have just mentioned. Never before have I feasted my eyes on such beautiful trees."

I quote this text in homage to this inspirational place, which has been ravaged several times by fire but has, since the dawn of time, embodied this poetry of wonderment. The Indians summed up the geological epic of Yosemite as a representation of "the earth's intelligence". Today, their children tell the story in the following way: "Five hundred million years ago, the sea that covered the region filled up with sediment. Two hundred million years ago, molten rock from below the earth's crust made its way to the surface following a neighbourhood quarrel between the plates of the North American continent and those of the Pacific. Enormous granite monoliths still bear witness to their struggle. Fifty million years ago, the region was a succession of hills covered with forests and criss-crossed by rivers. Three million years ago, a thick layer of ice covered the mountain, and the valley was widened considerably as a result of the glaciers moving through it. Ten thousand years ago, the glaciers retreated, leaving their moraine behind. Lakes appeared. Four thousand years ago, men settled in the valleys. About a hundred years ago, our ancestors were asked, under threat of military action, to go and settle elsewhere."

At Yosemite, granite and glaciers came together to form a valley with sheer rock cliffs of astonishing geometrical precision. The Merced River winds its way along the bottom of the valley at a height of some 1,200 m (3,936 ft), reflecting in its waters the surrounding greenery and steep rock faces.

Yosemite Falls, which can be seen from Glacier Point, thunder down from a height of 740 m (2,428 ft) into the more tranquil waters of the Merced River.

Yosemite National Park extends over an area of 3,080 km² (1,189 square miles). Yosemite Valley, in the southwest of the park, is the most beautiful and most visited area. Five hundred mature sequoias mount an impressive guard. The oldest of the giant sequoias in the Mariposa Grove is 2,700 years old; its branches are as big as the trunks of most trees. Mariposa Grove Museum has exhibitions devoted to the natural history of the region.

The part of Yosemite considered to be the wildest lies in the west of the park, in the great canyon of the Tuolumne River, where you might encounter marmots and mouflon. Stunning views are to be had at Glacier Point, with a sweeping panorama that includes El Capitan, the largest granite monolith in the world and still one of the ultimate tests for seasoned climbers. To the east, Yosemite Falls crash down in three stages from a height of 740 metres (2,428 feet). Late in the day the falls are transformed into a stream of molten silver dropping from the sky. The delicate tracery of rock on either side is suffused with a reddish ochre hue and, as the light fades away, the only remaining evidence of the waterfall's existence is the sound of its continuous pounding on the rocks below.

Standing here, it is not difficult to understand why men love rocks. Or perhaps it is not the rock itself that fascinates them, but rather the mystery of its mighty strength; the pre-human strength that it embodies.

Less famous than the trees in Sequoia Park's Giant Forest, the sequoias of Mariposa Grove include some splendid specimens, notably Grizzly Giant, the largest and oldest example of a species that has survived from the Mesozoic era.

Half Dome, a geological feature of relatively recent origin, is immediately recognizable by a wall of rock, 600 m (1,968 ft) in height, that splits the dome-shaped formation in half. It has become the emblem of the park.

*T*he sheer granite wall of El Capitan, the stuff of dreams for climbers all over the world,
extends 900 m (2,952 ft) upwards from the valley floor.

• John Muir •

Born in Dunbar (Scotland) on 21 April 1838, John Muir was to become the greatest American naturalist and pioneer of the battle to protect the environment. He was the inspiration behind the creation of America's national parks, and founder of the Sierra Club, the largest ecological association in America. However, his name remains associated above all with the protection of Yosemite Valley and it is due to his efforts that the valley is now considered one of the geological marvels of the world. Wisconsin prides itself on a Muir Lake and a Muir Knoll and there is a Muir Camp in Mount Rainier National Park in Washington State. *California Place News* claims he is the most commemorated person in the history of the state: there is Muir Wood National Monument in Marin County, Muir Gorge in Yosemite National Park, Muir Pass in King's Canyon National Park, Muir Crest and Muir Grove in Sequoia National Park, not to mention the John Muir Trail that winds along the mountains of the Sierra Nevada, John Muir College in Pasadena and Muir Station on the Santa Fe Railroad. He also has a species of butterfly, *Thecla muiri*, named after him.

Sequoia National Park, not far from Yosemite, is home to stands of giant sequoia; they owe their name not so much to their height – they are not quite as tall as their cousins the redwoods – as to their extraordinary girth. General Sherman Tree is 42 m (138 ft) in circumference.

The Grand Canyon is a place that defies all attempts at measurement. Geologically speaking, this natural barrier, one of the most formidable in the world, encompasses all the stages of the Earth's formation, from the Precambrian (two billion years ago) to the Tertiary period. The upper layer is made up of greyish-white limestone; below it come alternate, superposed bands of reddish-white sandstone, dark red and grey limestone, dull green shale, hard, dark brown gneiss, red granite, etc. More than 12 geological layers are visible in the Grand Canyon and these coloured formations are real works of art. There is in this monumental ornamentation a hidden element, a power both to calm and to intoxicate, a network of subtle inspirations that emerges out of the play of light on the bands of rock. The Colorado River has cut deep down into the rock of the high plateau which it flows across in its upper reaches, creating the series of 19 main canyons, including the Grand Canyon, through which it surges. The erosive power of the river is compounded by the action of rainwater and frost and the huge

The Grand Canyon cuts a dizzying gash 450 km (281 miles) in length in the Colorado Plateau. The difference in height between the top of its North Rim and the river below can be as great as 1,850 m (6,068 ft), while at its narrowest points it is only 200 m (656 ft) across. The walls of the Canyon bear witness to two billion years of geological, botanical, and zoological history recorded in their layers of schist, granite, gneiss, limestone, shale, and sandstone.

Francisco Vásquez de Cárdenas was the first white man to discover the canyon in 1540, but he failed to get down to the river. In 1776, the Franciscan Tomás Garces explored one of the tributaries of the river he named the Colorado (red river), but it was not until the end of the nineteenth century that the geologist and cartographer Wesley Powell made the first recorded trip through the canyons of the Colorado River itself.

quantity of snow that falls on the peaks in winter. This runoff water has also given rise to tributaries which in turn have sculpted side-canyons. The Grand Canyon is an open book revealing the geological history of the region. The fossils and composition of the various sedimentary layers, each of which represents a geological period, can be clearly observed. The whole harmonious combination is a subtle reminder that great beauty can flow from the ruin and destruction that inevitably accompanies all life on earth.

First, the jumble of rocks stretching away endlessly into a ferociously arid landscape, strewn with claw-like roots: a still life peopled only by vibrations. Then a succession of acropolises with white façades and unattainable ridges leaves the traveller alone in the silent immensity of the canyon, separated from the gods. What can the soul cling to in the chaos of the Colorado River? In the Grand Canyon, the eye rediscovers romantic inspiration as it bubbles up into the consciousness like a subterranean stream re-emerging into the open, permeated with the secret alchemy of the natural elements, an intoxicating combination of pure air, fluid

light and the red necklace of the river far below, which resembles a gigantic fertility symbol for a god of peace and forgiveness; a god capable of exploring the hidden face of the American night.

The tourist is well provided for at the Grand Canyon, but it remains a place where one has to leave the crowds behind in order to contemplate the great chasm in solitude. At any time of day, the glittering silence of the Grand Canyon can strike awe into anyone able to be of one mind with its red and blue land (for here even the sky is a physical presence). But be careful. Those unaccustomed to the rigours of life in the desert must understand that the obverse of awe and spiritual intoxication can be exhaustion. There is little shade in the canyon, and temperatures can be extreme. Always carry water, and wear a hat, sunglasses and sunscreen. The weather can also deteriorate rapidly, so never go into the canyon without adequate rain gear. All visitors should heed the advice given by rangers. The Grand Canyon of the Colorado River is one of the most formidable natural barriers in the world and must be treated with the respect it demands.

Maricopa Point is situated on a rocky crest which overlooks Indian Garden where the Havasupaïs Indians used to grow vegetables.

In the language of the Paiute Indians, former inhabitants of the region, the word "mountain" is a verb. At Bryce Canyon, this verb has a synonym: to sculpt. "The red rocks standing like men in a bowl-shaped recess," was how the Paiutes described the site. It is a surreal place, where spires and columns of glittering rocks display a whole palette of colours ranging from orange to dark red (iron oxide) to blue and even purple (manganese). Some of the spires are so delicate that they rise up in front of you like vibrating spears. At sunset, particularly when the bases of the raised rocks return once again to the shade, their upper parts seem to be lit by incandescent embers.

At Bryce Canyon, each hour of the day offers a new version of these metamorphoses. The most intense one takes place at midday, when the light beats down on the foot of the spires.

They seem almost to sway on their burning plinths. The Indians say that at that precise moment the light of the sky touches the earth. The spectator is taking part in a sacred performance, in which dead warriors enter the amphitheatre with its "meadows of rock". Masked

Vertical erosion reveals the various colours of the rock: iron oxide provides the red and orange hues, manganese oxide the blue and purple.

dancers rise up to challenge them. A terrible slaughter ensues, to which the red stains on the rocks bear witness even today.

Other legends refer to a secret alphabet that the gods, rushing to abandon the canyon before the white men arrived, are said to have scattered about before disappearing. And it is true that those with intuitive powers might detect a tremor of anguish, transformed into rock and standing on end like the hair on the earth's skull … For their part, the rangers speak of fairy chimneys, and this fairy-land of stone is indeed truly magical. And every visitor should pay silent homage to the amazing accomplishments of erosion, which has created the spectacle and spirit of Bryce Canyon.

The canyon was named after a pioneering couple, Ebenezer Bryce and his wife, who settled in the valley in the 1860s. Bryce built a house and a road along which he could take his timber out of the valley. In the 1880s, the couple left to settle in Arizona, but their daughter stayed behind. Later, when the man was asked what he thought of this Garden of Eden, he replied: "Well, it's a hell of a place to lose a cow in!"

• The national parks •

There are some fifty national parks scattered throughout the United States. The oldest of these is Yellowstone, which was declared a national park in 1872. The most recent are those in Alaska which were added to the park system in the late 1970s. Together, they occupy an area of more than 4 million hectares (15,440 square miles). An Act of Congress lays down standards for their protection and preservation.

A national park is a site of outstanding interest set aside for the preservation of natural features, as is the case with Yosemite, the Grand Canyon or Yellowstone, for cultural or historical reasons, as in the case of the Mesa Verde, which contains a remarkable historical legacy, or for a combination of these purposes. The parks are organized in such a way as to guide visitors and inform them of the cultural aspects and the particular characteristics of the sites. Guided itineraries are provided so that visitors can move about the parks in complete freedom, on condition that they respect the natural environment (hunting, fishing and the picking of flowers are prohibited or strictly regulated). Rangers are employed to supervise the national parks.

The base of Double Arch consists of soft red sandstone, formed from mud left behind by retreating seas; it is topped with a much harder sandstone known as slickrock.

To continue in the same vein, the names given to Delicate Arch, that marvel of geological sculpture, include such gems as "schoolteacher's knickers", "old girl's knickers" and "cowboy's chaps". These pearls of saloon-bar wit capture the very spirit of the pioneers who conquered the West …

Arches National Park, located in the eastern part of central Utah, covers an area of 296 km² (114 square miles) and lies at an altitude of between 1,200 to 1,700 metres (4,000 to 5,500 feet). Since its most distinctive characteristic is sandstone, I cannot resist the pleasure of quoting this passage from Victor Hugo: "Sandstone is the most amusing and most curiously shaped rock in the world. It is to rocks what the elm is to trees. There is no shape it cannot take on, no whims it does not have, no dreams it cannot give life to. Its countenances are many, its expressions varied. It seems quickened by a multiple soul. Forgive me the use of this word to describe an apparently inanimate substance.

In the great drama of the landscape, sandstone plays a fantastical role, sometimes haughty and severe, sometimes farcical. It leans over like a wrestler and curls up like a clown; it can be a sponge, a pudding, a tent, a hut, or a tree trunk; flaky, fawn-coloured hummocks might pop up here and there in the middle of a field of grass, or it might take on the shape of a herd of sleeping sheep; it has faces that smile, eyes that gaze, and jaws that seem to nibble and graze

on the heather; it seizes undergrowth like a giant's fist emerging suddenly from the earth. The Ancient Greeks, who liked extended allegories, should have used sandstone to make a statue of Proteus." Arches National Park illustrates perfectly the dialogue between image and the material world. There are no fewer than 500 natural arches in this petrified landscape. Some regard them as symbols of alliance or unity, while Indian legends speak of parts of an upturned vase and of the heat of the sun that warms that part of the eternal shattered by the white man. With this in mind, observe Delicate Arch or any of the other natural rock spans in the park as the sun rises, warming the stone with the heat of its rays. It is then that one dreams of a single human nature formed by forces at work deep within the Earth, just as the sun's rays seem to be seeking out an eternal, unifying truth from the Entrada sandstone created about 150 million years ago, during the Jurassic period, when layers of sand were deposited. With the passage of time, some have petrified, while others have been sculpted by water, sun, frost and wind, like signs of the enigma that the song of the blue rock thrush and the flight of the golden eagle also perpetuate in their own ways.

It is morning. The sun has not yet risen. It is cold. The words of the poet Baudelaire suddenly float into your consciousness: "Nature is a temple, where the living/Columns sometimes breathe confusing words;/Man walks within these groves of symbols, each/Of which regards him as a kindred thing." You begin to feel quivers of excitement; the key to the enigma seems finally within your grasp. In your mind, a curious presence begins to form whose movement, meaning and future emerge from matter itself. This is both a physical and metaphysical sensation. You prick up your ears to lie in wait for a pure melody as if, through the fabric of grey stones and the veil of night that is slowly lifting, the silence is finally going to answer, merging with the breath of the statues that haunt the landscape. The sun is just beginning to rise above Delicate Arch. Suddenly the light appears, and you allow your body to luxuriate in the delicious warmth of the first rays of the sun as they breathe new life into this great primeval landscape. For a brief, epiphanic moment, the mystery of the material world is revealed to you.

Delicate Arch is one of the most remarkable sights in the park. Its age is put at 70,000 years and its life expectancy at a further 15,000 years.

Lake Powell is an artificial lake whose history has a genuinely epic quality. The first Europeans known to have written about the region were two Spanish priests, Fathers Escalante and Dominguez, who went on an expedition to explore the area in 1776. Less than a century later, Captain John Wesley Powell took up the torch again. After the Civil War, he became a government adviser on ecological matters, which he analysed as a scientist aware of the enormous energy resources harboured within the Colorado River. In 1867 and 1868, J.W. Powell mounted two expeditions in preparation for the adventure he had been toying with for a long time, namely the exploration of part of the basin of the Colorado River, which he undertook in May 1869. A journey of some 1,700 kilometres (1,062 miles) was to take him, in 98 days, from Green River (Wyoming) to the confluence of the Virgin River, through Canyon Lands, then Glen Canyon and finally the Grand Canyon – the greatest challenge of all.

Glen Canyon Dam was part of a project developed between the two World Wars with the aim of stabilizing the erratic course of the Colorado River. Congress gave the go-ahead in 1956 and the dam was completed in 1966. However, although Glen Canyon began to be submerged as early as 1963, the 650 km² (250 square miles) of Lake Powell were not completely filled until 1980. It forms one of the most beautiful landscapes in the Far West.

The waters of the lake abound in perch, trout, catfish, pike and giant carp, and there are more than 200 species of birds on the shores of the lake. In spring, those shores are carpeted with lilies, lupins, primroses, and wild rhubarb; in the rest of this particularly arid region, the only plants that grow are cacti, yucca, and sagebrush …

Lake Powell is always a very impressive sight, all the more so since the total length of its perimeter (3,500 km/2,188 miles) is greater than that of the Pacific seaboard of the United States (3,100 km/1,937 miles). It is a popular summer destination for Americans, despite the extreme heat. Their favourite excursion is to Rainbow Bridge – a trip of 160 kilometres (100 miles), which can be done by boat in a day.

The shores of Lake Powell (total circumference 3,500 km/2,188 miles) emphasize the contours of the numerous side-canyons of Glen Canyon that were submerged under 150 m (492 ft) of water from 1963 onwards.

The West Mitten megalith in Monument Valley is undoubtedly the most frequently filmed and photographed landscape in the whole world.

Harry Goulding and his wife Mike were the first white people to settle in Monument Valley in 1923. Having opened a trading post and then an inn, they invited John Ford to visit the place. He filmed *Stagecoach* here in 1938, the first in a series of westerns shot in Monument Valley.

Monument Valley covers an area of 120 km² (46 square miles); its otherworldly landscape consists of mesas transformed by the forces of erosion into distorted, monumental shapes. The Navajo used to live here in huts about 8 metres (26 feet) in diameter known as hogans. The circular shape of the hogans reflected their belief in a world that was circular, like the sun and the moon, and cyclical, like the changes of the seasons. The door of a hogan always opened to the east.

Among the Navajo, the origin of weaving is attributed to the Spiderwoman, a mythical holy woman. According to legend, this holy woman lived in a secret cave in the Canyon De Chelly, in what is now Arizona. The spiders' webs were the manifestations of her exceptional skill in the art of weaving, and the hands of the skilful

The hieratic Totem Pole, 120 m (394 ft), presides as master of ceremonies over Navajo dancers.

Navajo weavers were guided by her spirit. However, her mythical genius depended on natural laws linked directly to the powers of the sun and the thunder – her first web was woven on an imposing loom forged by flashes of lightning and the rays of the sun.

Monument Valley inspires immense reverence. As Longfellow wrote, "a pure will inundated our world. One could hear the breath of air that brings fertility."

The winds here will keep your eyelids open, in a state between rapture and somnolence. You can wander between Sentinel Mesa, Mitchell Mesa, and West Mitten Butte, which looks for all the world like a finger pointing skywards and, before going to sleep, recite to yourself the enigmatic words of the poet Guillevic:

"One evening

When everything will be purple in the universe

And the rocks will resume their crazy trajectories

They will awake."

Since 1987, visitors to Monument Valley have been unable to depart from the marked routes. In order fully to appreciate the Valley's beauty, visitors have to hire the services of a guide or win the friendship of an Indian who may offer you a guided tour of his lands.

The Canyon De Chelly belongs to the Navajo people, and their traditional dwelling, the hogan or "earth igloo", can still be seen, although most Indians have abandoned them for more comfortable mobile homes.

• From cowboys to westerns •

In 1830, the first meaning of the word "cowboy" was horse thief. By 1850, it had come to mean "ordinary cattleman", and over the next 20 years his reputation improved still further as cattle breeders gradually gained control over the Indians' hunting grounds. At that time, herding the cattle along the trails was a veritable epic and became the stuff of legend – a vital source of the myth of the "Wild West" that grew up between the Midwest and the Pacific. The coming of the railway in 1865 hastened the colonization that sounded the death-knell of Indian power. General Sherman's "pacification" put an end to the rearguard action fought by the Sioux (marked by the surrender of Sitting Bull in 1881) and confined the survivors to reservations. In 1877, the uprising of Chief Joseph's Nez Percés, together with that of the Dakotas in 1890, marked the final convulsions of the Indian Nations of the Far West. After that, the cowboy had the vast space of the American West, both real and symbolic, to himself; his domination of it was further consolidated by authors such as Ernest B. Maycox and Stuart N. Lake in *My Darling Clementine* and *Stagecoach*.

• The bison •

In 1800, there were more than 60 million American buffalo, more properly called bison, living in wild herds on the Great Plains. During migrations, vast numbers of animals would move in dense waves stretching over dozens of kilometres. The Indians took from the bison what they needed to satisfy their basic needs. A report by a member of the seventeenth-century Coronado expedition shows how the animal was integrated into their way of life: "The Indians live on the bison because they do not grow corn. They use its hide to make houses. They also use it to clothe and shoe themselves and twist strands of it together to make ropes. They use its hair in place of wool. Its tendons are used to make thread with which they sew their clothes and tents. They fashion tools from its bones and burn its excrement as fuel for lack of firewood. The Indians cut the flesh of the bison into thin strips, which they dry in the sun. Once dried, the meat is ground into flour, which makes it easy to transport and to convert, when required, into a sort of gruel or porridge that is cooked in a pot that they always carry with them. This bison meat flour swells up so much that a single handful is enough to make a whole pot of porridge." In order to get close to the herds of bison that roamed the Great Plains, Indian warriors would usually camouflage themselves beneath wolf skins in order to outwit the animal. The Indians believed that the skins conferred on them both bravery and speed. On the other hand, the painter George Catlin, writing in 1851, left us a striking description of this battle to the death between man and beast: "The Indians' favourite quarry is the bison, which is almost always hunted on horseback, with bows and arrows and spears. Their horses are small but very agile. They capture them on the Plains, where they live wild in large herds. On his little wild horse, which he trains for several years, the Indian hunter rides full tilt into the middle of the herds of bison. The horse is the fastest animal on the Plains and it takes its rider without difficulty right up to the bison, which at such close range is an easy target for his deadly weapons … The horses are trained in such a way that their riders scarcely need to use reins, which hang over the horse's neck as he approaches the bison from the animal's right-hand side. The rider can then fire his arrow into the bison's left flank just as he draws level with the animal's heart, striking it a mortal blow as the arrow sinks in up to the flight." Generally, when the hunter was pursuing a large herd, he would stick close to it until he had selected a beast and would then isolate his quarry as quickly as possible by placing himself between it and the rest of the herd. Once he had directed his horse towards the animal he had picked out, he would strain every sinew to get as close as possible, giving the horse its head and carrying his tautened bow low against the horse's left flank. As soon as he had drawn level with the bison, he would lean over to one side and fire the arrow. The horse, which was instinctively afraid of the bison, would have its eyes riveted on the furious beast just in front of it and, as soon as the critical distance had been reached, would swerve away, whether its rider had fired or not … Nevertheless, however careful the rider and however crafty the horse, terrible collisions did take place, since the excitement of the chase was often so great that neither instinct nor reason could prevail. On occasions, both horse and rider hurtled to their deaths. During the hard winters, the Indians put on snowshoes which enabled them to walk over the snow while the heavy bison sank into it, making them easy prey for the hunters. By about 1870, as the white colonization advanced, there were only some 13–15 million bison left on the Great Plains. Their systematic destruction then began – to such an extent that by the end of the nineteenth century there were only one million left, barely enough to ensure the survival of a species that is now protected.

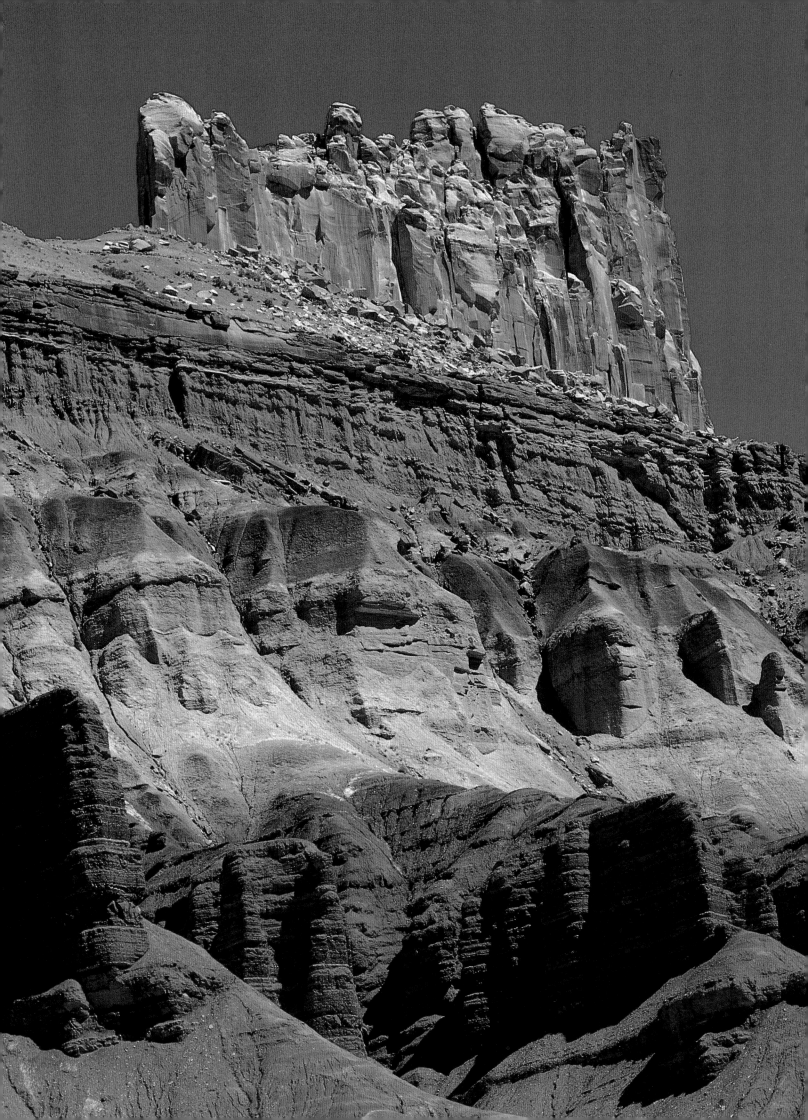

The Reef, whose golden hue calls to mind the domes of American state capitols,
forms a cliff overhanging geological formations
coloured by bentonite and petrified wood.

• Go West •

By about 1850, disputes with the Indians centred more on the price of horses than on territorial problems. Rather than Indian arrows, it was disease, exhaustion, drownings, and madness that marked out the thousands of kilometres leading to Eldorado. Numerous skeletons lined the trails leading westwards, and messages for those who would follow were carved into the skulls of cattle that had died of exhaustion. The journey across Utah and Nevada was particularly arduous. And crossing Death Valley was akin to a rite of passage that, for some, fed the myth of a promised land and a new life. The ever-increasing numbers of fortune-seekers and the regular encroachment by white men on Indian hunting grounds very quickly poisoned relations. Indians would slip into encampments by night and spirit away horses and cattle. It was not long before the first shots rang out and a covert war replaced the fragile equilibrium between the communities. The road to the West became a route to be feared, particularly since the Indians were quick to mobilize on a warlike footing. Those in charge of the wagon trains often preferred to try to cross Indian territory under cover of darkness.

Canyonlands, which was promoted to national park status in 1964, lies at the heart of Canyon Country, a landscape sculpted into a fantastic labyrinth of chasms and fissures by the Colorado and Green Rivers. The strangeness of the landscape is the expression of natural forces that have been at work for several million years. Eroded walls, bare mesa tops, deep ravines and striated crevasses chiselled out of the rock, massive screes, and rock falls: the whole landscape is a jumbled mass of rock that is still being pierced and whittled away by the indefatigable force of the water. To the north, the plateau known as Island in the Sky offers the most spectacular panoramas, notably Dead Horse Point, a promontory once used as a paddock for wild horses all of which, sadly, died of thirst and neglect. At the Maze, the intricate tangle of canyons, where Butch Cassidy once found refuge, becomes inextricable, although two trails, reserved for seasoned guides, cross the rough, uneven terrain. To the southeast loom the Needles: access by car is easier, but anyone seeking initiation into the mysteries of Canyonlands should consider hiking through this fantastic landscape.

*T*he plateau of Island in the Sky
rises up in the north of Canyonlands
National Park, dominating the
surrounding region and offering
the most spectacular viewpoints,
particularly at Green River Overlook.

Death Valley owes its name to a tragedy that occurred at the time of the Gold Rush. On Christmas Day 1849, about 100 men, women and children turned off the usual route to the Californian gold fields to take what they thought was a shortcut through the desert valley. They went through a hell of thirst and starvation. One of the party who had gone to look for help, an army captain called Culverwell, did not return. Because they could not agree on the route, the rest of the party divided into six groups and finally escaped, although by then they were reduced to emaciated, skeletal figures.

Death Valley is one of the hottest regions in the world. In summer, the temperature can reach 57° C (134° F) and in winter can go as low as –10° C (14° F). In the ice age, Death Valley, which is sheltered from the influence of the Pacific Ocean, was filled by a lake 190 kilometres (120 miles) long and surrounded by mountains. After this first lake had disappeared, another lake gradually formed. This one also dried out, leaving behind a thick layer of mud made up of

After a great deal of tectonic and volcanic activity, the retreating sea left behind alluvial basins, as here at Zabriskie Point. The region has rich deposits of precious metals and talc.

borax – a mixture of boron and sodium or calcium plus water – and salt. Innumerable small clumps of this mud line the bottom of the valley and sparkle in the sunlight.

Despite these extremely difficult natural conditions, there has been a human presence in the valley for over 9,000 years. Four different cultural groups have lived in the valley since the Nevares Springs settled here in the seventh century BC. Shoshone Indians were living in the valley when the pioneers arrived. At the end of the nineteenth century, the Shoshones were adherents of a religion centred around the Ghost Dance, the dance of the spirits that heralded the arrival of an Indian messiah. Indeed, since the white man had killed Jesus the Messiah, His successor would necessarily be an Indian, particularly since, in a trance-like state during an eclipse of the sun in 1888, a certain Wovoka, subsequently known as the Paiute Messiah, had made contact with God, who asked him to preach love and peace. "Do not fight any more. Do not do harm to anyone. Do right always. Do not tell lies. When your parents and your friends die, you must not weep."

His preachings took root firstly among the Shoshones and Bannocks and then the Crows before reaching the northeast of the United States. The Cheyenne, the Arapohs, the Wichitas, and related tribes were seized by an intense fervour. They danced until they fainted. Having regained consciousness, they would tell of their meetings with dead ancestors and friends. Gradually, a vague hope that the Indian land would be reborn crystallized into a conviction. This new earth would bring with it the messiah, their dead ancestors and friends, newly returned to life, and the wild animals. And this stream of people and animals would push the white men back to the East and hurl them into the sea. A date was even set for the fulfilment of this prophecy: the spring of 1891, when the grass was one inch high.

In 1891 the American Army, warned of the unrest that was sweeping through the Indian reservations, was prepared for any eventuality. Spring came. The grass quickly grew to a height of one inch, but deliverance did not come. The Ghost Dance ended in a second defeat and cruel disillusion.

The landscape is still being shaped by volcanic activity: Ubehebe Crater is only a few hundred years old.

In the Valley of Fire, the fractures in the Earth's surface are so vast that the tangle of rocks and strata eludes analysis by even the most experienced of geologists.

The geological history of the Valley of Fire in the state of Nevada has been linked with that of neighbouring Grand Canyon since the early Precambrian period. At the time when the Laramie Mountains were being formed by intense upward displacement, it was the difference in the thickness of the Earth's crust that decided their fate: instead of being raised up by the thrust of the Pacific tectonic plate, as at the Grand Canyon, the thinner crust at the Valley of Fire was folded into an apparently inextricable tangle of rock strata and fault fractures. Wind erosion then sculpted the immense arches of red sandstone, such as Aztec Arch, Whimsical Arch, Table Arch, and Elephant Rock, that tower up against the cobalt sky like totemic figures. The Valley of Fire deserves its name: flames seem to shoot out from all sides as the rocks change colour. At Silica Dome, near Lake Mead, the range of colours becomes more subtle as ravines of yellow and fawn-coloured sandstone alternate against a backdrop of mist-shrouded mountains. And in winter, when the dormant plants glisten with an almost phosphorescent greyish-blue colour against the glimmering red earth, the Mojave desert resembles a strange lunar garden.

• The pioneers •

When gold fever had abated, the fortune-seekers discovered the real treasures of the West, particularly the fertility of the soil. Because of its agricultural value, ownership of the land became a real issue. There were three distinct waves of settlers. Like the gold diggers, trappers were mainly adventurers living on the margins of society. They were followed by squatters – colonists who, having cleared some land, sold it on ready for cultivation. The third wave, made up of farmers seeking to settle in the region, also attracted shopkeepers, craftsmen, priests, doctors and teachers. In 1862, the Homestead Law allowed any man of full age to settle on a plot of federal land on payment of a modest fee. After farming the land for five years, ownership of the plot reverted to the farmer at no further cost. However, the promised land did not always live up to expectations. The colonists often fell prey to unscrupulous businessmen, and they also had to do battle with the Indians who were violently opposed to the constant encroachment upon and continuous reduction of their lands. By about 1890, however, the West was no longer either "far away" or "wild". The frontier had ceased to exist.

The early French pioneers called them "the lands that are bad to cross". They have become the Badlands National Park, in the state of South Dakota. The park covers an area of almost 1,000 km^2 (400 square miles); it lies in an arid region of sedimentary rock covered with moss and short grass with outcrops of pink or grey sandstone, rounded by glacial action in some places and bristling with jagged ridges in others. From a distance, this rocky landscape looks as though it has been woven and worn down by time, layer after layer. It is not difficult to imagine the distress of the pioneers searching for fertile land when they came across this no man's land, where their wagons could only bump over rock. At that time, the Badlands were surrounded to the east by the mythical Great Prairie, with its bison and Sioux Indians led by Chief Big Foot and to the west by the Black Hills, which lie at the foot of the Rockies and were still haunted by the legendary figures of Jesse James, Calamity Jane and Wild Bill Hickok. Nevertheless, from the nineteenth century onwards palaeontologists discovered the largest collection of fossils in North America in some extremely curious rock strata

uncovered by erosion. In the Big Badlands, at the northeastern entrance to the park, the remains of a Brontotherium, the largest mammal known to have lived in America, were dug up. Hundreds of millions of years ago, the Badlands were covered by a sea, as is shown by the marine fossils, particularly those of tortoises, found in the stratum of black shale formed by sedimentation. Forty million years later, during the Oligocene epoch, the golden age of mammals, the sea had retreated and the climate of the Badlands was tropical, causing the area to be covered in lush vegetation. Then the climate became drier and the Badlands turned into a region of savannah that was home to herbivores such as rhinos, hippopotamuses, camels, and horses. At the same time, the land gradually became covered with volcanic ash from neighbouring volcanoes. As it weathered, this ash mixed with the shale to form a friable, spongy clay compound known as bentonite, which is very widespread in the Western Badlands. When wet, this substance swells to eight times its original volume; when it dries out, it loses all consistency.

The Badlands harbour the largest collection of fossils in North America.

In the Black Hills south of Rapid City, the faces of Washington, Jefferson, Lincoln and Roosevelt have been carved into the granite of Mount Rushmore. The sculptures, 20 m (65 ft) high, were created between 1927 and 1941.

• God bless America •

Weakened by the war with Mexico, America was looking for fresh money. Recession was looming and industrialization needed fresh impetus. The East Coast was clogged with thousands of immigrants who had to have concrete incentives before they would rush to conquer the continent. At that time, the Union had only five member states west of the Mississippi: Texas, Louisiana, Arkansas, Missouri and Iowa. These five states accounted for 90 per cent of the two million people who made up the population of the western territories.

Politically, California was not yet officially American, although it had been under the protection of an American military governor for two years. However, the 3,589 tonnes of gold it produced every year (the world total was 12,303 tonnes) were to become an engine of economic growth and ultimately make the USA a world power. By a strange acceleration of the historical process, Mexico was to sell California for 15 million dollars on 2 February 1848, barely ten days after the first gold nuggets had been discovered on 24 January 1848. Two years later, this newly acquired American state was to produce three times its purchase price in gold ingots.

The 381 km² (147 square miles) of the Petrified Forest National Park offer travellers an opportunity to go back 225 million years in time, and to walk in a park of mariposas, cactuses, and sunflowers. The park also contains one of the largest concentrations of fossils in the world. The origins of this extraordinary landscape go back to the end of the Triassic period, when immense pine forests were buried under volcanic mud and ash following a cataclysm. The absence of oxygen prevented the wood from decomposing and the wood cells filled up with silica. After the wind had swept away the surface sediment and dried up the lake, the petrified forest was exposed to the light of day.

The Petrified Forest National Park is a reminder that the dynamic relations between the elements remain a mystery and that the metamorphoses wrought by time can emerge as clusters of reflections the colour of the dawn. Visitors to the park will find the petrified logs laid out in a sort of primordial jumble. Here, nature has become a vast panorama in which the god of images has installed his works like rosaries summoning up a lost Atlantis.

Wood becomes mineralized in two ways. In one, dissolved wood is replaced by various forms of chalcedony, including jasper, carnelian and agate. In the other, quartz fills the tiny cells of the wood and gradually crystallizes.

The cactus is the king of the desert plants and is the symbol of the state of Arizona. The saguaro (Carnegia gigantea) *can reach a height of 17 m (56 ft); during rainstorms, it is capable of taking up several tonnes of water in just a few hours.*

The Sonoran Desert has been used in many westerns when directors wanted shots of the sun setting behind the giant saguaro cactus, which has branches like a candelabra. This famous cactus gives the area around Tucson a soul, an identity, and an aesthetic force that were dear to Yves Berger: "Here they are, throwing out two, three, four, even five crooked arms, bolted to the upper part of a deeply grooved body that, from the ground to its very tip, is planted with little warts from which the spines emerge. A famous variant has two atrophied arms, as if the plant had been struck by phocomelia following an injection of thalidomide. This variant is so often reproduced, so often seen that if the species were to die out with the last saguaro, it would remain in the memory for ever. Like stone, it is emblematic and it already borders on the mythological. I have seen some that had a sort of headdress of five or six cacti, like a queen wearing a crown or a tribal chief his crest, and others that produced stumps of cactus projecting from their stems: seen from a distance, they looked like animals running over the spines. Amazing. And again, from a distance, there are slopes and hills

Depending on altitude and position, cactuses flower from February to October, with a peak period between April and June.

completely covered in hundreds and thousands of cactuses that look as if they are bristling with matches. What joy!"

Among many other unexpected animals, the Sonoran Desert is home to the roadrunner, that curious bird, a wide-awake, hyperactive member of the cuckoo family, noted for its swiftness of foot and star of many a Warner Brothers cartoon, in which it pokes fun at the coyote with its incessant loud bleeping. Rather than flying, the roadrunner walks with a comic military gait through the desert, chasing lizards and rattlesnakes and using its long tail as a rudder to make sudden about-turns.

*I*n good years, when the rains come,
the Sonoran Desert in spring is
ablaze with an extraordinary
display of blossom.

Organ Pipe Cactus National Park is home to a wide range of cactuses, including the senita, the saguaro, and the organ pipe itself.

• The friend of the Indians •

"Savages we call them, because their manners differ from ours, which we think the Perfection of Civility; they think the same of theirs. [...]

The Indian Men, when young, are Hunters and Warriors; when old, Counsellors; for all their Government is by the Counsel or Advice of the Sages; there is no Force, there are no Prisons, no Officers to compel Obedience, or inflict Punishment. Hence they generally study Oratory; the best Speaker having the most influence. The Indian women till the Ground, dress the food, nurse and bring up the Children, and preserve and hand down to Posterity the memory of Public Transactions. These Employments of Men and Women are accounted natural and honorable. Having few Artificial Wants, they have abundance of Leisure for Improvement by Conversation. Our laborious manner of Life compared with theirs, they esteem slavish and base; and the Learning on which we value ourselves they regard as frivolous and useless."

Benjamin Franklin (1784)

The dunes in White Sands National Monument are as white as snow.

*T*he sand, composed largely of gypsum, may reach a height of several hundred metres.

*The draconian measures taken by the park authorities are intended
to preserve a landscape where only the wind leaves its mark.*

• John August Sutter •

Sutter, a Swiss disciple of Jean-Jacques Rousseau, set up a community in the Sacramento Valley in California inspired by the philosophical principles of the Enlightenment. There were neither rich people nor poor people in "New Helvetia". He himself struck coins that could be exchanged for goods on sale in the community shops. The workers in the mills, sawmills and workshops where the giant trees of the region were sawn up were mostly ship's carpenters, helmsmen or boatswains who had jumped ship after having been promised five dollars a day. He handed out land or gave work to the poor Russian, Irish and German settlers who showed up on his doorstep, attracted by the community's fame and prosperity. One morning in 1848, one of them, a man named Marshall, discovered several large nuggets of gold in the balancing reservoir of a sawmill that he himself had built. The whole country was gripped with a manic obsession with power and wealth. In just a few months, Sutter's community had imploded and California was seized by capitalist hysteria. The Gold Rush had begun.

Plants grow to unusual sizes in order to stop themselves sinking into the sand.

White Sands is in the state of New Mexico, the largest of the states in the southern part of the Far West. New Mexico covers an area of 315,000 km² (121, 590 square miles), but has a population of little more than 1.5 million, since it is essentially a huge desert. Once a cattle-rearing state, it now attracts many tourists.

White Sands, which lies between Alamogordo and Las Cruces, is a desert of dazzling white gypsum dunes. Indian legends speak of "white walls of birds slain by lightning".

As the sun sets, the lengthening shadows create fantastic shapes, like the swaying of wings above the void. White Sands is a solemn place, vulnerable to desecration, where nature seems to have whited out its own memories. Standing here is like being in the middle of an unbroken ocean – one longs for escape from the monochrome uniformity that stretches out like the seamless dress of a sleeping goddess.

The further one walks towards the centre of the dunes, the scarcer the plants become. The emblematic plant here is the agave, the leaves of which are used to produce sisal and the fermented juice

to make mescal. And the reddish-brown bushes of the creosote plant are a good match for the orange-pink veil that spreads across the dunes at sunset, imparting a faint glow to the landscape that, paradoxically, intensifies the whiteness even as it softens it. Even the animals that live here – the Apache pocket mouse, the bleached earless lizard and the pronuba moth that infests yucca plants – are white, as if they had been blinded by so much immaculacy and had merged with the colour of the gypsum in order to escape predators. One has to go to the edge of the dunes in order to find the coyotes, kangaroo rats, bobcats, hares and owls that also inhabit these white deserts.

In the southwest corner of Utah, sheer sandstone cliffs rise up dizzyingly along the Virgin River. Ponderosa pines cling to each rocky escarpment and, at the bottom of the canyon, elders, ash trees and poplars enliven the river. Zion National Park has something of that Arcadian atmosphere that delights all travellers.

The white-tailed hare and the large-eared deer meet here for never-ending discussions. For their part, the kingfishers, kestrels, jays and bluebirds seem to be deciphering a score by Olivier Messiaen.

In autumn, the choruses begin with a soft murmuring. Along the edges of the woods, above the "emerald pools" shrouded in wisps of fog, a spluttering of metallic notes can be heard. Lower down, near the river, an incessant chattering, which seems to be sung, spoken and whistled all at the same time, betrays the presence of the blackbird. The orchestra gradually builds up. The first rays of sunlight in the cold morning air bring forth songs of joy from the throats of the birds. Their wings, still sluggish with the cold, begin to quiver with the joy of being together and sharing the same life and the same soul …

At the foot of the White Cliffs flows the Virgin River. Many of the place names here, such as Temple of Sinawava, West Temple or Altar of the Sacrifice, are religious in inspiration …

The combined erosive power of wind and water lays bare the various rock strata. Following pages: the road that runs through the park towards Bryce Canyon passes through some truly magnificent geological formations.

• John James Audubon •

Audubon was born in Louisiana in 1785, the son of a French shipowner from the Sables d'Olonne who was engaged in the slave trade. He was to become a brilliant naturalist and a highly skilled animal illustrator. His masterpiece, *The Birds of America*, is made up of 435 folio plates depicting 1,065 birds life-size. At the age of 58, having travelled through the southeast and then the north of the United States, and just as he was beginning the first illustrations for *The Viviparous Quadrupeds of North America*, he went on an expedition to Yellowstone. In fact, he was saying a final farewell to a region he loved passionately: he knew he was ill, and he also realized that the Western America he loved was already doomed. A friend of the Indians, he said that the wilderness was "the state of creation closest to divine perfection: the Earth, fresh from the hands of God, for nothing is more perfect than the original". He died in 1851, after having published some scientific notes and memoirs. He was a man of great sensitivity who, throughout his life, showed a deep love of nature and a particular fondness for birds.

• Legendary figures •

The first of these legends was Daniel Boone (1734–1820). Born in Pennsylvania, he explored eastern Kentucky with five companions between 1769 and 1771, going deep into what the Indians called the "dark, bloodstained lands". A friend of the Indians, he could travel in the wildest country without ever getting lost. In 1775, the territory he had explored became part of Virginia before forming the state of Kentucky.

Chronologically, the second legendary hero was Davy Crockett (1786–1836), whose courage was equalled only by his complete lack of learning, of which he boasted. This lack of education did not prevent him from becoming a member of the US Congress following a turbulent election campaign. Historians have cast doubt on many of the tales of his exploits, and in particular on the one he used to tell about how he killed 105 bears in a year, for the simple reason that Davy Crockett could only count to one hundred! Towards the end of his life he went to Texas to join the struggle against Mexican rule. He is said to have been the last of 184 soldiers to die defending the Alamo at San Antonio.

Kit Carson was born in 1809 in Kentucky. He is considered a worthy rival to Daniel Boone. A skilful diplomat, he was also a crack marksman who has an enduring place in the mythology of the West as the real upholder of the law on the prairies.

The one sheriff in the West who could not be ignored was Wild Bill Hickok (James Butler Hickok, 1837–1876). He began to be widely talked about through his activities as an outlaw. It was during this period that he acquired the nickname "Wild Bill". He was also a particularly skilful buffalo hunter and passed his knowledge on to Buffalo Bill. He obtained his first sheriff's badge at Fort Riley (Kansas), which he rid of outlaws before pursuing an exceptional career that took him to Hays City in Kansas and then to Abilene. A firm-handed sheriff, Wild Bill was also a noted dandy: it was said that the embroidery on his jackets could deflect pistol bullets! According to William B. Kearns: "The grips of his two Colt 44s were decorated with mother-of-pearl." He never walked anywhere but in the middle of the road in order to be able to deal with any attack. There is a story that, on being attacked one day by six men, he had drawn his gun and killed two of his attackers before the others had had time to fire a single shot. Nevertheless, he was killed by a certain Jack McCall, a hired gun working for a band of outlaws from Kentucky.

However, the most celebrated of all these legendary figures was Buffalo Bill. An intrepid scout in the prairies, an unerring marksman and a superb horseman, William Frederick Cody (1846–1917) also had an exceptional ability to detect and follow Indian tracks. His nickname reflected his skill in killing bison: in one eighteen-month period, Buffalo Bill killed 4,280 bison with his famous Springfield carbine.

In 1872, after a journalist had written about his exploits, a play entitled "Buffalo Bill, the King of the Westerners" brought him on to the stage, where he played himself. The play was a success, and eventually became Buffalo Bill's Wild West Show, which opened at New York's Bowery Theatre. The show was a triumph, and toured for 35 years all over the world, including 6 years in Europe.

Once he had returned to the USA, Buffalo Bill, haunted by the memory of his successes, took his Wild West Show on tour again; in 1905, he was in Paris, encamped on the Champ de Mars, near the Eiffel Tower. Unfortunately, this revival was not as successful as he had hoped and he returned once more to America. He fell ill while playing another part in the Miller brothers' circus (Ranch 101) on tour in Omaha. He died on 10 January 1917 and was buried with much ceremony on the top of Lookout Mountain, which dominates the town.

PLANNING YOUR JOURNEY

TOURIST INFORMATION: American Travel and Tourist Board (Visit USA Association) Tel. 0891 600 530. For specific information on the National Parks, there is a National Park Service: P.O. Box 37127, Washington D.C. 20013, Tel. 001-202-3434621.
The Internet address of the National Park Service is: http://www.nps.gov.
More detailed information on the National Parks in the North-West can be obtained from the Outdoor Recreation Information Center, 83, S. King Street, Suite 212, Seattle, Washington 98104, Tel. 001-206-4425565. For the Rocky Mountains: National Park Service, P.O. Box 25287, 12795 West Alameda Parkway, Denver, Colorado 80225-0287, Tel. 001-303-9692500. Information on the National Parks in the South-West can be obtained from: National Park Service, P.O. Box 728, 1100 Old Santa Fe Trail, Santa Fe, New Mexico 87504-0728, Tel. 001-505-9886004. For the West and California, write to: National Park Service, Fort Mason Building 201, San Francisco, California 94123, Tel. 001-415-5560560.

TRAVEL FORMALITIES: British citizens travelling to the United States no longer need a visa for a stay of up to 90 days. A valid passport and a return air ticket are all that is required.

AMERICAN EMBASSIES AND CONSULATES:
– London: American Embassy, 24 Grosvenor Square, London W1A [Tel. 0171 499 9000].
– Edinburgh: American Consulate-General, 3 Regent Terrace, Edinburgh EH7 [Tel. 0131 556 8315].
– Belfast: American Consulate-General, Queens House, Queens Street [Tel. 328239/242520].

BRITISH EMBASSIES AND CONSULATES IN THE USA:
British Embassy: 3100 Massachusetts Avenue, NW, Washington D.C. 20008, Tel. 001-202-5886500, Fax 001-202-5887870.

There are also Consulates-General in Los Angeles and San Francisco and a Consulate in Seattle.

CURRENCY: The currency is the American dollar (1 US $). $1 = 100 cents. There are six coins: 1 cent (penny), 5 cents (nickel), 10 cents (dime), 25 cents (quarter) and 50 cents and $1. Quarters are the most useful coins, since they can generally be used for telephones, parking meters and other slot machines. Banknotes (bills) exist in the following denominations: $1, $2, $5, $10, $20, $50 and $100. Be careful: they are all the same colour and so are easily confused. Credit cards are the most common method of payment for travellers in the USA. The most frequently used cards are American Express, Diners Club, MasterCard (Eurocard) and Visa. The Eurocheque card is virtually useless. Traveller's cheques in US dollars are also widely accepted in payment for goods and services. Foreign currency can be exchanged at airports and at some banks in large towns (they are generally open from 9 a.m. to 3 p.m., Monday to Friday). However, travellers are advised not to bring foreign currency to the United States, since the exchange rate is unfavourable and foreign-exchange bureaux are virtually non-existent in US cities.

INOCULATIONS/HEALTH: No inoculations are currently required for travellers entering the USA from Europe. The health care system in the USA is very good but very expensive. Treatment must be paid for directly; in most cases, payment can be made by credit card. Travel insurance providing an adequate level of cover for health care costs is essential.

CUSTOMS: In addition to personal baggage, the following items may be brought in duty-free: goods to the value of $100, 200 cigarettes and 1 litre of spirits or 2 litres of wine. Cash in excess of $10,000 must be declared.

GETTING THERE: Air connections to the United States are very good. Many American airlines work closely with their European counterparts and offer special deals. Peak season is from mid-June to mid-August. Outside this period, prices are considerably lower. The main airlines include Air Canada, American Airlines, British Airways, Continental Airlines, Delta Airlines, KLM, Lufthansa, Northwest Airlines, TWA, United and USAir. Many companies operate non-smoking flights.

USEFUL FACTS ABOUT THE USA

GEOGRAPHY: The USA stretches right across North America from the Atlantic to the Pacific, covering an area of some 9.4 million km² (3.62 million sq. miles). The capital city is Washington D.C., which has about 630,000 inhabitants.

TYPE OF STATE: Federal state, constitution adopted in 1787.

CLIMATE: The states on the northern Pacific coast have a damp, cool climate. The south-western states have a dry, continental climate, while the climate in the northern Rocky Mountains similar to that of the Alpine regions of Europe. California is divided into two quite distinct climatic zones: the cool, rainy north and the hot, dry south. Colorado, Utah, Arizona and New Mexico have a desert climate.

LOCAL TIME: The USA crosses a number of time zones. The Western states (e.g. California) are in the Pacific Time Zone, which is 8 hours behind Greenwich Mean Time (GMT). The Mountain Time Zone (e.g. Arizona) is 7 hours behind GMT.

In summer, however, Arizona is on the same time as California and Nevada, but one hour behind Utah, Colorado and New Mexico, because it does not go onto daylight-saving time (except for the Navajo Reservation). In winter, Arizona is one hour ahead of California and Nevada, but the same as Utah, Colorado and New Mexico.

ECONOMY: The USA is a highly industrialized country and one of the most important trading countries in the world.

POPULATION: 74% white, 11% Afro-American, 9% Hispanic, 3% Asian, 0.8% Native American, 2.2% others. The total population of the USA is 253 million.

RELIGION: Predominantly Protestant, but also Catholic, Jewish, Orthodox, Old Catholic and Buddhist.

LANGUAGE: English.

WEIGHTS AND MEASURES: Temperatures are expressed in Fahrenheit (68°F = 20°C), distances in miles and weights in pounds. Capacity is measured in gallons, but beware: the US gallon is only 0.833 of the UK gallon.

TRAVELLING IN THE USA

TRANSPORT: In such a huge country, flying is a very common mode of travel. Some of the large American airlines offer travellers on their transatlantic flights special discount tickets for travel between US destinations. Such tickets can be purchased only outside the United States. Smoking is forbidden on domestic flights.

Those not put off by the uncomfortable seats of Greyhound buses can travel right across the USA on them. This bus company offers travellers the Ameripass, which gives unlimited travel for a single price and can be bought in advance for periods of 7, 15, 30 or 60 days. The Amtrak train network is not very extensive, providing links between major cities only. There are no train stations in the National Parks, except in Glacier National Park. Some lines cross the entire continent from East to West. Journeys on historic railways are popular.

HIRING A CAR: If you want to be independent, you can hire a car, motorcycle or motor home. Bookings can be made before you leave for the USA. The minimum age for hiring a vehicle is between 21 and 25, and at least one year's driving experience is required. An international driving licence is recommended. The hire cost usually includes "collision damage waiver", which releases the person hiring the car from liability for damage to the car they are driving. However, further insurance may be required for third party cover, known as "full collision waiver". You will be offered a choice of several different kinds of car: economy (2 seats), compact (4 seats), mid-size (5 seats), full-size (6 seats) or mini-van (7 seats). They will all have air-conditioning. The minimum hire period is 4–7 days. The hire charge includes unlimited mileage. You do not need a special licence to hire a mobile home (recreational vehicle, or RV). There are generally three models available, offering space for between 2 and 6 people.

THE ROAD SYSTEM: The road system is a little different from that in Europe. "Highways" are the equivalent of our trunk roads, while "expressways" or "freeways" are motorways through or bypassing a city. "Interstate highways" are the equivalent of our motorways; when they become "toll roads" or "turnpikes", then a toll is charged. Roads are designated by the letters US followed by an odd number for those running North–South and an even one for those running East–West. You will not find destinations marked on American roads, just a road number followed by the geographical direction (N, S, E, W). The rules of the road are essentially the same as in Great Britain, although there are some significant differences. In many states, for example, it is permissible to turn right at red lights, provided the way is clear. And on dual-carriageway roads, it is permissible to overtake vehicles on either side. Speed is restricted to 20 to 25 mph in urban areas and to between 55 and 65 mph on highways. These limits are generally observed and enforced.

ACCOMMODATION: There are many hotel chains in the USA, some of them covering the whole country. Motels and hotels are of international standard and usually have air-conditioning. Most of the big chains have a toll-free central reservation service. Many hotels will not hold reservations after 6 p.m. unless you have given advance notice of a late arrival. There are also many bed and breakfast establishments now in America. Another option is staying on a ranch, for which addresses can be found in the "Farm Ranches and Country Vacations" guide. Those who prefer to camp or who have hired an RV will find a wide choice of camp-grounds or trailer parks. It is often not possible to make advance reservations, so it is advisable to start looking for a site early in the day.

PRACTICAL TIPS: If you intend to use electrical equipment, such as razors or hairdryers, of non-American manufacture, you will need both a 110-volt transformer and a plug adaptor with two flat, parallel pins. It is a good idea to keep a supply of $1 bills to hand for tips. Give bellboys in hotels one dollar for each item of luggage they carry for you and the chambermaid one dollar for each day of your stay. Waiters and taxi-drivers expect tips of between 10 and 15% of the bill.

THE NATIONAL PARKS

There are altogether 54 national parks in the USA, more than half of which are in the 11 western states. Taken together, the National Parks cover an area of about 350,000 km² (135,000 sq. miles). There are visitors' centres in each national park where information can be obtained. The infrastructure in the parks is generally good, and includes campsites or accomodation in hotels. There are usually shopping facilities as well. Depending on the location, there may be opportunities for mountain climbing or hiking, back-packing, fishing, skiing, jeep trips and sometimes wild water rafting. Entry to the National Parks costs between $5 and $10, while the Golden Eagle Pass for $25 gives entry to all the National Parks at no further cost.

ROCKY MOUNTAIN NATIONAL PARK (Colorado): The small town of Estes Park is the more easterly of the two entrances to this park, which covers an area of almost 1,000 km² (386 sq. miles) and is open all year round. The highest mountain in the park is Longs Peak, which stands at a height of 4,345 metres (14,250 feet). It is one of the biggest tourist attractions in the USA, and has more than 3 million visitors every year. Trail Ridge Road runs through the park, but is open only from the end of May to mid-October. Breathtaking views can be had from Many Parks Curve and Rainbow Curve. There are some 568 kilometres (350 miles) of hiking trails in the park. Rock Cut is the starting point of the Tundra Nature Trail, which runs across the tundra above the tree line. In the south-western section of the park is the largest natural lake in Colorado, the Grand Lake, which is the highest stretch of water used for recreational sailing in the world. Lake Granby is an artificial lake, considerably bigger than Grand Lake.

OLYMPIC NATIONAL PARK (Washington): The park occupies virtually all the Olympic Peninsula and is bordered to the west by the Pacific ocean. The area is dominated by Mount Olympus, 2,428 metres (8,000 feet) in height; its upper slopes are surrounded by ice fields and glaciers, while its lower slopes are covered by rain forests with gigantic Douglas firs and other huge conifers. The park is open all year round and can be reached by Highway 101, which virtually encircles the entire area. A beautiful footpath to the scenic Marymere Waterfalls, almost 30 metres (100 feet) in height, begins at the Storm King Visitor Center.

YELLOWSTONE NATIONAL PARK (Wyoming): The first park of its kind to be established in the world, with a surface area of almost 9,000 km^2 (3,500 sq. miles), Yellowstone is the biggest national park in the USA and the largest animal reserve after Alaska. The Yellowstone River flows through Yellowstone Lake, the largest mountain lake in America. Upstream of the lake, the river flows through Yellowstone Canyon, which is almost 300 metres (1,000 feet) deep in places. The area is famous for its geysers, hot springs and mud volcanoes. The most famous geyser is Old Faithful, which shoots hot water almost hourly to a height of nearly 60 metres (200 feet). At Mammoth Hot Spring, there are hundreds of hot springs, which have deposited terraces of gleaming white limestone. The park has five entrances, 800 kilometres (500 miles) of road and 1,600 kilometres (1,000 miles) of footpaths. One of the main roads is the Grand Loop Road, 235 kilometres (146 miles) in length, which loops across the park in a figure of eight. The fauna in the park is typical of the Rocky Mountains. There are brown and grizzly bears, bison, wapitis, elk, fish and 200 different species of bird. The park is open from May to October inclusive. There are organized events from mid-June to mid-September only.

CRATER LAKE NATIONAL PARK (Oregon): Not far from Klamath Falls, this is the only national park in Oregon. It is accessible all year round and, with an area of around 649 km² (250 sq. miles), is relatively small. A road about 50 kilometres (30 miles) long leads to the edge of the crater, which stands 600 metres (1,965 feet) above the midnight-blue waters of the lake. The lake, the deepest in the USA at almost 590 metres (2,000 feet), came into being around 7,000 years ago when Mount Mazama was split asunder by an eruption. Wizard Island, a volcanic plug 200 metres (650 feet) in height, rises out of the middle of the lake like a magician's hat. The visitor center is in Rim Village, on the south-west corner of the lake.

YOSEMITE NATIONAL PARK (California): Named after an Indian tribe and founded in 1890, Yosemite is one of the most beautiful and most frequently visited of the national parks. Two rivers, the Merced and Tuolumne, flow across the park. It covers an area of some 3,000 km² (1,150 sq. miles) and has imposing Alpine peaks, magnificent waterfalls and splendid forests of sequoias. Near the western entrance is Yosemite Valley, the most beautiful part of the park. The granite monolith of El Capitan rises almost vertically above the Valley. At Mariposa Grove, two miles away from the southern entrance, stand the most magnificent sequoias, including Grizzly Giant, which is almost 3,000 years old. There are two distinctive mountains near Yosemite Village, where there is also a visitor center: Half Dome and the three peaks known as Three Brothers. Here you will find the most beautiful waterfalls, including Yosemite Falls, one of the highest in the world at almost 750 metres (2,500 feet). The roads are usually passable all year round, although Tioga Road, which runs from east to west, is closed from November to May.

GRAND CANYON NATIONAL PARK (Arizona): This park was founded in 1919 and covers an area of 4,930 km² (1,900 sq. miles). Over a period of millions of years, the Colorado River has cut a 450-kilometre (280-mile) long gash in the southern part of the Kaibab Plateau. A helicopter flight over the canyon gives passengers an opportunity to admire a breathtaking spectacle of colours and shapes. Those in good physical condition can use old trails winding along its steep walls to explore the canyon on foot or on mules. It is also possible to go down the Colorado River on rafts or rubber boats. Owing to the great differences in height, a range of climatic zones exists within the canyon, from desert to temperate. In the eastern part of the park, it is possible to drive from viewpoint to viewpoint between Desert View and Grand Canyon Village all year round. One of the most famous views is that from Mather Point. The western section between Grand Canyon Village and Hermit's Rest is closed to private cars

during the summer and accessible only by shuttle buses. The
North Rim of the Grand Canyon is closed from mid-October to
mid-May, because of frequent snowfalls. There are Indian
reservations very close to the canyon.

BRYCE CANYON NATIONAL PARK (Utah): This canyon is on the
eastern edge of the Paunsangunt Plateau, which stands about
2,500 metres (8,200 feet) high. It is about 145 km² (56 sq. miles)
in area, and is named after a pioneer couple who settled here in
1860. Bryce Temple, Gulliver's Castle, Cathedral and Chinese
Wall are just some of the formations, reminiscent of cities and
bizarre spires, shaped by erosion.

ARCHES NATIONAL PARK (Utah): This park is in a
desert region in the heart of Canyonlands and
covers an area of almost 300 km² (115 sq.
miles). It is named after the 80 or so
fantastically shaped natural arches created
out of reddish sandstone, of which
Landscape Arch in Devil's Garden,
89 metres (292 feet) in height, is
the mightiest in the whole
world. Delicate Arch, though
smaller - at a mere 26 metres
(85 feet) - in height is in a more beautiful position. There are
also many other bizarre rock formations in the park, resembling
battlements, towers and windows.

LAKE POWELL (Arizona): This artificial lake came into being when
the federal government built the mighty Glen Canyon Dam
across the Colorado River. It has a perimeter of some 3,200
kilometres (around 2,000 miles), making it a paradise for
aficionados of water sports. Rainbow Bridge, the largest natural
stone bridge in the world and a holy place for the Navajo
Indians, is a popular destination for excursions.

MONUMENT VALLEY (Utah): This valley, which covers about 2,250 km² (870 sq. miles) of the Colorado Plateau, is famous from countless movies. It became a protected area in 1960. Route 163 leads from Kayenta straight through the Valley, past imposing, free-standing red rock monoliths, with evocative names such as Elephant Butte, Thunderbird Mesa and Totem Pole. There are also guided tours in four-wheel-drive vehicles, as well as flights over the valley.

CANYON DE CHELLY (Arizona): The name of this park, which covers an area of 336 km² (130 sq. miles), is derived from the Navajo word "tsegi", meaning "rock canyon". Some of the most interesting sights in the canyon are the cliff dwellings, of which there are about 100 dating from between 350 and 1300 AD. The most famous are Mummy Cave, White House and Antelope House. Spider Rock is a monolithic pinnacle of red sandstone whose sheer walls rise 245 metres (800 feet) from the canyon floor. Navajo Indians still live in the canyon today.

CAPITOL REEF NATIONAL PARK (Utah): This national park, almost 1,000 km² (390 sq. miles) in area, has a vast sandstone reef, 105 kilometres (65 miles) long and 300 metres (985 feet) high,

which has Indian petroglyphs from the 9th to 12th centuries carved into it. Magnificent natural bridges, monoliths and other rock formations, such as The Castle, Twin Rocks and Chimney Rock, can be viewed against the backdrop of the Fremont River.

CANYONLANDS NATIONAL PARK (Utah): This park, which lies on both sides of the Colorado River, around the mouth of the Green River, is made up of several imposing, wild canyons. The whole landscape has been sculpted by erosion into a bizarre jumble of needles, bridges and mesas. A good road leads into the northern part of the park, the Island in the Sky plateau, where there is a visitor center. From there, the road goes south to Grand View Point Overlook, which offers spectacular panoramic views.

DEATH VALLEY NATIONAL MONUMENT (California): Death Valley is a low-lying stretch of desert between the Panamint Range to the west and the Amagosa Range to the east. The Valley, which is around 225 kilometres (140 miles) long and 20 kilometres (12 miles) wide, came into being as a result of tectonic activity. In the distance, across dried-out salt lakes and sand dunes, rises the snow-capped Telescope Peak. Temperatures in summer can reach 57° C (134° F). Death Valley is open all year round.

VALLEY OF FIRE STATE PARK (Nevada): Petroglyphs created by Anasazi artists can still be seen on the almost sinister sandstone formations of the Valley of Fire. The stone shimmers in all possible shades of red and brown, so much so that at sunrise and sunset it seems almost to be on fire.

BADLANDS NATIONAL PARK (South Dakota): The Badlands are a high plateau, almost 1,000 km^2 (390 sq. miles) in area; the landscape is composed of furrowed slopes, angular mountains, deep, many-branched ravines and shaped rock formations.

MOUNT RUSHMORE NATIONAL MONUMENT (South Dakota): The stone guardians of Mount Rushmore were carved into the granite cliff between 1927 and 1941. The artist then died and the portraits of four presidents (Washington, Jefferson, Lincoln and Roosevelt) remain unfinished. The memorial is less than 3 kilometres (2 miles) from Keystone and is open all year round.

PETRIFIED FOREST NATIONAL PARK (Arizona): The largest of the petrified logs, which are more than 225 million years old, can be seen in Jasper Forest; in other parts of the park, all sorts of plant fossils are to be found. At Puerco Indian Ruins, you can see the homes of the people who created the petroglyphs that are still visible at Newspaper Rock. In the northern section of the park, various overlooks offer sweeping views of the colourful lowlands of the Painted Desert.

SONORA DESERT (California and Arizona): The Sonora Desert lies in the rain shadow of the Californian Sierra Nevada. The many-branched saguaro cactus is the most characteristic of the plants found in this wonderful desert landscape; capable of surviving harsh conditions for more than 150 years, it has become the symbol of the desert.

WHITE SANDS NATIONAL MONUMENT (New Mexico): Near Alamogordo, in the middle of a military testing zone, lie the glistening dunes of White Sands. They consist of crystallized gypsum and can be up to 20 metres (65 feet) high. The park is open from the end of May to the beginning of September.

ZION NATIONAL PARK (Utah): This rocky valley is 24 kilometres (15 miles) long and in places almost 900 metres (3,000 feet) deep. The Virgin River has created a landscape of bizarre rock formations. One of them is the Great White Throne, 750 metres (2,460 feet) high, while the Temple of Sinawawa is a natural theatre. This national park is open all year round, although guided tours take place only from the end of May to the beginning of September.

ADDRESSES OF THE NATIONAL PARKS

ARCHES NATIONAL PARK
P. O. Box 907
Moab, Utah 84532
Tel: 001 801 259 8161
Fax: 001 801 259 3411

BADLANDS NATIONAL PARK
P. O. Box 6
Interior, South Dakota 57750
Tel: 001 605 433 5361
Fax: 001 605 433 5404

BRYCE CANYON NATIONAL PARK
Bryce Canyon, Utah 84717-0001
Tel: 001 801 834 5322
Fax: 001 801 834 4102

CANYON DE CHELLY
P. O. Box 588
Chinle, Arizona 86503
Tel: 001 520 674 5500
Fax: 001 520 674 5507

CANYONLANDS NATIONAL PARK
125 West 2nd South
Moab, Utah 84532-3298
Tel: 001 801 259 7164
Fax: 001 801 259 7164

CAPITOL REEF NATIONAL PARK
P. O. Box 15
Torrey, Utah 84775-9602
Tel: 001 801 425 3791
Fax: 001 801 425 3026

CRATER LAKE NATIONAL PARK
P. O. Box 7
Crater Park, Oregon 97604
Tel: 001 541 594 2211

DEATH VALLEY NATIONAL MONUMENT
Death Valley
California 92328
Tel: 001 760 786 2331

GRAND CANYON NATIONAL PARK
P. O. Box 129
Grand Canyon
Arizona 86023
Tel: 001 520 638 7888
Fax: 001 520 638 7797

LAKE POWELL
Glen Canyon National
Recreation Area
P. O. Box 1507
Page, Arizona 86040
Tel: 001 520 645 2433

MONUMENT VALLEY
Monument Valley Tribal
Supervisor
P. O. Box 93
Monument Valley
Utah 84536
Tel: 001 801 727 3231

MOUNT RUSHMORE NATIONAL
MONUMENT
P. O. Box 268
Keystone
South Dakota 57751
Tel: 001 605 574 2523
Fax: 001 605 574 2307

OLYMPIC NATIONAL PARK
600 East Park Avenue
Port Angeles
Washington 98362
Tel: 001 360 452 7949

PETRIFIED FOREST NATIONAL PARK
P. O. Box 2217
Arizona 86028
Tel: 001 520 524 6228
Fax: 001 520 524 3567

ROCKY MOUNTAIN NATIONAL PARK
Estes Park
Colorado 80517-8397
Tel: 001 970 586 9308
Fax: 001 970 586 1310

WHITE SANDS NATIONAL MONUMENT
P. O. Box 1086
Holloman AFB
New Mexico 88330
Tel: 001 505 479 6124
Fax: 001 505 479 4333

YELLOWSTONE NATIONAL PARK
P. O. Box 168
Yellowstone National Park
Wyoming 82190
Tel: 001 307 344 7381
Fax: 001 307 344 2005

YOSEMITE NATIONAL PARK
P. O. Box 577
Yosemite National Park
California 95389
Tel: 001 209 372 0200
Fax: 001 209 372 0333

ZION NATIONAL PARK
Springdale
Utah 84767
Tel: 001 801 772 3256
Fax: 001 801 772 3426

Date of publication: November 1997.
All information has been carefully checked.
However, no guarantee can be given as to its accuracy.